# CHEERLEADING CAMPS

Leah Kaminski

www.av2books.com

Published by AV2 by Weigl
350 5th Avenue, 59th Floor
New York, NY 10118
Website: www.av2books.com



Library of Congress Cataloging-in-Publication Data

Names: Kaminski, Leah, author.
Title: Cheerleading camps / Leah Kaminski.
Description: New York, NY : AV2 by Weigl, [2020] | Series: Cheerleading |
Audience: Grades: K-3. | Includes index.
Identifiers: LCCN 2019012100 (print) | LCCN 2019016811 (ebook) | ISBN 9781791109882 (Multi User ebook) |
ISBN 9781791109899 (Single User ebook) | ISBN 9781791109868 (hardcover : alk. paper) |
ISBN 9781791109875 (softcover : alk. paper)
Subjects: LCSH: Cheerleading--Juvenile literature. | Sports camps--Juvenile literature.
Classification: LCC LB3635 (ebook) | LCC LB3635 .K35 2020 (print) | DDC 791.6/4--dc23
LC record available at https://lccn.loc.gov/2019012100

Printed in Guangzhou, China
1 2 3 4 5 6 7 8 9 0  23 22 21 20 19

052019
103118

Project Coordinator: Heather Kissock
Designer: Ana Maria Vidal

Every reasonable effort has been made to trace ownership and to obtain permission to reprint copyright material. The publishers would be pleased to have any errors or omissions brought to their attention so that they may be corrected in subsequent printings.

Weigl acknowledges Getty Images, iStock, Shutterstock, and Alamy as its primary image suppliers for this title.

# CHEERLEADING CAMPS

## Contents


AV[2] Book Code .......... 2

The World of Cheerleading Camps .......... 4

History of Cheer Camps .......... 6

Cheer Camps Timeline .......... 8

How Cheer Camps Work .......... 11

Cheer Camp Athletes and Coaches .......... 12

The Right Tools .......... 14

The Right Moves .......... 16

Getting Involved .......... 18

PROFILE: CheerAbility .......... 20

Quiz .......... 22

Key Words/Index .......... 23

Log on to www.av2books.com .......... 24

# The World of Cheerleading Camps

Cheerleading camps are incredibly intense and very fun. Also called clinics, cheer camps often run for several days. Cheerleaders stay overnight. There are day camps, too. Campers try new **stunts**, dances, and cheers. There is always an emphasis on safety. Campers also learn about being strong performers.

More than half a million cheerleaders attend camps every year in the United States.

Cheerleading camps are most popular for high school **squads**. There are also camps for college and middle school teams. There are even teams for youth cheerleaders. Squads usually attend camp as a team. Camp helps them prepare for the next season.

Bonding exercises are an important part of camp. Campers do scavenger hunts. They give each other fun nicknames. Bonding helps teams cheer better together. There are many fun cheer camp traditions. These include door decorations and **spirit sticks**.

Before camps began, cheerleaders practiced after class during the school year.

# History of Cheer Camps

The history of cheer camps includes many organizations. Lawrence “Herkie” Herkimer started one. It is the National Cheerleaders Association (NCA). He did this in the 1940s. The NCA started cheerleading camps. Only 52 girls and 1 boy went to the first camp. At the next camp, there were 350 cheerleaders. NCA camps focus on cheers and stunts. They also work on perfecting techniques.

Jeff Webb now runs 4,000 camps each summer.

Jeff Webb started the Universal Cheerleaders Association (UCA). This was in 1974. UCA camps focus on complicated pyramids and **acrobatics**. UCA has had a big influence on modern cheer. In 1979, a classic stunt was first done at UCA camp. It is now called the basket toss.

UCA offers a special program. It is the Varsity Spirit/NFHS Squad **Credentialing** Program. This program teaches cheerleaders about safety. It is now part of all UCA camps.

## SPIRIT STICKS

In 1954, Lawrence Herkimer was at an NCA camp. He noticed one cheerleading squad. The squad did not have the best techniques. Its members worked hard. They encouraged others. Herkimer wanted to reward their spirit. He painted a small tree branch and awarded it to them. He called it a "spirit stick." The spirit stick is now an important tradition for cheerleaders. Many squads sell spirit sticks in team colors to raise money.

# Cheer Camps Timeline

Cheerleading camps started more than 70 years ago. Since then, they have become popular in the United States. There are thousands of camps for cheerleaders.

Early cheer chants included team and school names. Over time, chants have become more like short songs.

**1948** Lawrence Herkimer runs the first cheerleading camp. It takes place at Southern Methodist University in Texas. Herkimer had graduated from the college earlier that year. He studied science.

**1975** UCA teachers lead a college camp in Memphis, Tennessee. They perform the first cheer routine set to music.

**1984** By the mid-1980s, at least 150,000 girls attend U.S. cheer camps each year.

**1999** Cheerleading camp sizes almost triple in 15 years. At least 400,000 cheerleaders go to U.S. camps in 1999.

**2000** A cheerleader is hurt at a cheer camp. He wins an important court case in Montana. The decision guides many other cases on cheer safety. It leads to extra supervision and medical care for cheerleaders across the country.

**TODAY** UCA is the largest cheer camp company in the world. It trains more than 180,000 cheerleaders every summer. UCA offers about 3,200 camp sessions each year.

Golden Empire Youth Tackle Football and Cheer is a large camp in Southern California. It is for ages 6 to 14.

# How Cheer Camps Work

In addition to the UCA and NCA, schools and cheer teams hold cheerleading camps for themselves. Some camps are private. Others are open to the public. There are camps for every age, ability, and **specialization**.

At a standard overnight camp, campers eat breakfast together. They get an early start on a full day. They often take classes after dinner, too. A camp might include many classes. Classes are in dance, stunts, and jumps. Cheerleaders might also have one-on-one instruction. They also receive performance **evaluations**. No matter what, a cheerleader is expected to show his or her positive spirit while at camp. Many camps end with an awards ceremony. Some of the most important awards are for spirit.

Lawrence Herkimer sold his camp business in 1986. He made **$20 million.**

Some camps include a talent show. Campers show off what they have learned in classes.

# Cheer Camp Athletes and Coaches

Many people help camps run well. Camp instructors are usually experienced cheerleaders. They often cheer for colleges and universities. Instructors are **mentors** to the younger cheerleaders. They show campers new moves. Instructors also let the campers know how they are doing. Before camp starts, instructors help create new stunts. They also learn cheers, stunts, and dances to teach campers.

Instructors keep campers on beat by counting out loud. The eight-count is common in cheerleading. Instructors call out, "1, 2, 3, 4, 5, 6, 7, 8!" in perfect time.

Team coaches often go to camps as well. They may even take classes themselves. A cheerleading squad at a camp might include **rookies**. It also might include experienced members. This includes squad captains.

Many large camps have tryouts for instructors. Tryouts test their cheer techniques and speaking skills.

# The Right Tools

Cheerleaders want a successful camp experience. This requires packing the proper items. A cheerleader can talk to his or her squad about what to bring.

**Notebook and Pen** A notebook and pen or pencil are crucial at camp. Cheerleaders use them to write down routines and cheers. They can practice them later.

**Water Bottle and Sunscreen** Camps are often held outside in the summer. Cheerleaders need to take care of their bodies throughout camp. A water bottle and sunscreen can help.

**Team Clothing** Squads often wear the same outfits for the first day of camp. They bring team uniforms and accessories. Comfortable athletic clothes in team colors are also needed.

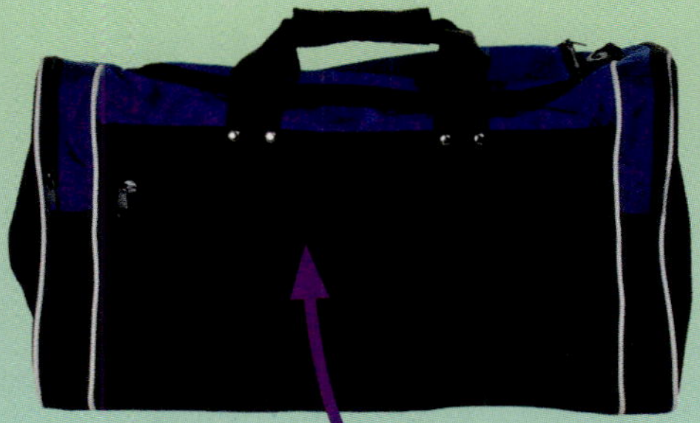

**Overnight Bag**
It is important that campers bring basic items. They need toothbrushes and pajamas. They can pack a favorite pillow and blanket, too. These items can help young cheerleaders feel better when they are away from home.

# The Right Moves

At cheerleading camps, attendees often learn new moves. Campers also build on previous skills. There are a few moves that cheerleaders can expect to see at camp.

**Cartwheel** In a cartwheel, athletes begin in a front **lunge**. Then, they pitch forward. Both hands are put on the ground sideways. Legs are kicked over the body. The body twists to the side. Feet land one foot at a time.

**Spread Eagle** The spread eagle is a type of jump. First, cheerleaders jump straight up. Then, the legs are spread wide. Arms are spread up in a high V. The body looks like the letter X.

**Awesome** In a stunt called the awesome or cupie, teammates lift a **flyer**. The flyer then stands straight. His or her feet are together. The arms are stretched up to form a V.

**Arabesque** In the arabesque, the flyer kicks one leg backwards. The leg is held out. It is parallel to the ground. The chest and head face forward. Arms can then be stretched out. The body forms the letter T.

# Getting Involved

Cheer camp is a great way to build team **unity** and individual skill. There are many different options for cheer camps. Whichever you choose, make sure it will help you move toward your cheerleading goals.

**1.** Choose between a day camp or an overnight camp. Overnight camps are the most popular option. You can also consider a day camp. Day camps are held by local sports associations or schools.

Choreography camps usually last two or three days. Squads learn routines that match their strengths.

**2.** If you are on a cheerleading squad, think about your team's goals for next season. Are you beginners? If so, consider a general cheerleading camp. Are you ready to work on more specific skills? A stunt camp or **choreography** camp might be better.

**3.** After you have chosen a camp, you may need to raise money. Money pays for travel and fees. There are many fun options for raising money. Your team can provide a service. Try hosting a car wash and charging money. You can create and sell calendars. You could run a fashion show and take donations for entry.

**4.** An overnight camp might be too far away. Contact UCA or NCA. Ask if they can create a camp near you. Overnight camp might be too expensive for your team. You can ask your coach to run a day camp at your school.

## GOAL SETTING

Setting goals can help you get the most out of cheer camp. You can set personal goals. You can also set goals with your squad. The best goals are specific and can be measured. One example is a personal goal to master a cartwheel. Another is a team goal to get into a pyramid five seconds faster. Before camp, write down your goals. You can review your goals later at camp. This will help you stay focused.

# CheerAbility

Everyone can cheer, and there are camps for everyone. Cheerleading is a growing sport. **Accessible** cheer camps are becoming more common.

CheerAbility is in Franklin County, Virginia. It is one of many cheer camps that focus on cheerleaders with disabilities. Brittany Yates was named Ms. Wheelchair Virginia in 2014. She founded the camp in 2014. Yates had the help of a local company.

Many large competitions have divisions for cheerleaders with disabilities. Camps help the cheerleaders prepare for competition.

CheerAbility campers are young people who use wheelchairs. They do not focus on what they cannot do. They learn to take advantage of what they can do. A cheer squad from a local college volunteers to instruct the campers. They teach campers many different cheers and chants.

Campers use **pom-poms** given to them by the camp. These pom-poms are stamped with the camp motto. They say, "Adapt. Believe. Compete." CheerAbility allows kids to make friends and learn valuable cheerleading skills.

Cheerleaders use pom-poms to attract the crowd's attention. Many cheerleaders practice with pom-poms at camp.

# Quiz

**1** What are cheer camps also called?

Clinics

**2** Who founded the Universal Cheerleaders Association?

Jeff Webb

**3** In which year did Lawrence Herkimer run the first cheerleading camp?

1948

**4** How do many cheer camps end?

With an awards ceremony

**5** Are most camp instructors coaches?

No, they are experienced cheerleaders.

**6** What do squads often wear for the first day of camp?

The same outfits

**7** Which letter does the body look like in the spread eagle move?

X

**8** In which year did Brittany Yates found CheerAbility?

2014

# Key Words

**accessible:** easily used by any person

**acrobatics:** gymnastic moves that require balance and skill

**choreography:** how performers move during a routine, usually set to music

**credentialing:** getting a document or license that lets a person do a certain job

**evaluations:** reports on how well a person does a task

**flyer:** a cheerleader who is held up or tossed into the air when doing stunts

**lunge:** a move during which the front leg is forward and the body is lowered with knees bent

**mentors:** people who are experienced and teach younger people

**pom-poms:** large tufts of colored ribbons with handles

**rookies:** people who are new to a sport

**specialization:** an area of knowledge from extra training and practice

**spirit sticks:** long, thin sticks or batons often decorated with ribbons and streamers

**squads:** cheerleading teams

**stunts:** advanced cheerleading moves during which cheerleaders are held up or tossed in the air

**unity:** working together and getting along well

# Index

arabesque 17
awesome 17

bonding 5

captains 13
cartwheel 16, 19
CheerAbility 20, 21, 22
choreography 18
classes 11, 13
coaches 12, 13, 19, 22

goals 18, 19

Herkimer, Lawrence "Herkie" 6, 7, 9, 11, 22

instructors 12, 13, 22

National Cheerleaders Association (NCA) 6, 7, 11, 19

pom-poms 20, 21

safety 4, 7, 9
spirit sticks 5, 7
spread eagle 16, 22
stunts 4, 6, 7, 11, 12, 17, 18

Universal Cheerleaders Association (UCA) 7, 9, 11, 19

Yates, Brittany 20

# Log on to www.av2books.com

AV² by Weigl brings you media enhanced books that support active learning. Go to www.av2books.com, and enter the special code found on page 2 of this book. You will gain access to enriched and enhanced content that supplements and complements this book. Content includes video, audio, weblinks, quizzes, a slideshow, and activities.

## AV² Online Navigation

**Audio**
Listen to sections of the book read aloud.

**Book Pages**
AV² pages directly correspond to pages in the book.

**Video**
Watch informative video clips.

**Embedded Weblinks**
Gain additional information for research.

**Key Words**
Study vocabulary, and complete a matching word activity.

**Try This!**
Complete activities and hands-on experiments.

**Quizzes**
Test your knowledge.

**Slideshow**
View images and captions, and prepare a presentation.

**AV² was built to bridge the gap between print and digital. We encourage you to tell us what you like and what you want to see in the future.**

**Sign up to be an AV² Ambassador at www.av2books.com/ambassador.**

Due to the dynamic nature of the internet, some of the URLs and activities provided as part of AV² by Weigl may have changed or ceased to exist. AV² by Weigl accepts no responsibility for any such changes. All media enhanced books are regularly monitored to update addresses and sites in a timely manner. Contact AV² by Weigl at 1-866-649-3445 or av2books@weigl.com with any questions, comments, or feedback.